Y0-ABA-604

FAITH JOURNAL

This Journal Belongs to

_____

Starting Date: _____

End Date: _____

INTRODUCTION

Why Journal?

Journaling is a way of recording and keeping track of your encounters with God during your daily quiet time with Him and His Word. If you've never journaled before, as you spend time in the Word and in prayer, you will discover that it can help you learn how to listen for, and more clearly recognize, the voice of the Holy Spirit as He ministers to you.

God loves you, and is always ready and waiting to talk with you about anything and everything. Whatever is important to you is important to Him as well, because you're precious to Him. He has a specific plan for your life. He wants to tell you about that plan, and lead you through it step by step. The more you learn to hear His voice, the more you will be able to follow His promptings and walk the path He has charted for you. "My sheep hear My voice, and I know them, and they follow me." (John 10:27)

How to Use This Journal

This *Faith Journal* has several sections in it that you can utilize as you see fit. There is a Prayer List section where you can record your prayers and indicate when you've received answers. There is also a Bible Reading Checklist you can use to track your progress as you journey through the various books. Use the Daily Entries pages to record your thoughts and any scriptures that speak to your heart as you study your Bible.

Begin your Bible reading with prayer, such as: "Open my eyes that I may see wonderful things in your law" (Psalm 119:18). The Bible is God's Word. Ask God to teach you and speak to you through His Word. When you hear from Him, dare to take each faith step He puts in front of you. Each one you take will bring you closer to becoming what He has purposed for you to be, and to accomplishing what He has planned for you to accomplish, all for His glory.

In the future, maybe even years from now, when you look back on these pages you will see in them how far you've come—and how God has spoken with you, led you, counseled you, answered your prayers, and helped you grow spiritually and fulfill His purpose for you specifically.

How to Use the Bible Reading Checklist

The Bible Reading Checklist, located at the back of your journal, lists the books of the Bible, along with their corresponding chapters. Although the books are listed in the order in which they appear in the Bible, you don't have to read them in sequence. However you decide to proceed, as you finish each chapter of a book, place a checkmark or an "X" over it to cross it off the list. When you complete a book, draw a line through it. This will help you keep track of your progress through the Bible.

DAILY ENTRIES

This is what the LORD, the God of Israel, says:
"Write in a book all the words I have spoken to you."
Jeremiah 30:2

DATE: _____

Scripture/Subject _____
_____

My Thoughts _____
_____
_____
_____
_____
_____
_____
_____
_____
_____
_____
_____
_____
_____
_____
_____
_____
_____
_____
_____

Faith Step for Today _____
_____
_____
_____

Scripture/Subject _____
_____

My Thoughts _____
_____
_____
_____
_____
_____
_____
_____
_____
_____
_____
_____
_____
_____
_____
_____
_____
_____
_____
_____

Faith Step for Today _____
_____
_____
_____

Yet to all who received him, to those who believed in his name,
he gave the right to become children of God...
John 1:12

DATE: _____

Scripture/Subject _____
_____

My Thoughts _____
_____
_____
_____
_____
_____
_____
_____
_____
_____
_____
_____
_____
_____
_____
_____
_____
_____
_____
_____
_____
_____
_____

Faith Step for Today _____
_____
_____
_____

Scripture/Subject _____
_____

My Thoughts _____
_____
_____
_____
_____
_____
_____
_____
_____
_____
_____
_____
_____
_____
_____
_____
_____
_____
_____
_____
_____

Faith Step for Today _____
_____
_____
_____

It is Jesus' name and the faith that comes through him
that has given this complete healing to him, as you can all see.
Acts 3:16

DATE: _____

Scripture/Subject _____
_____

My Thoughts _____
_____
_____
_____
_____
_____
_____
_____
_____
_____
_____
_____
_____
_____
_____
_____
_____
_____
_____
_____

Faith Step for Today _____
_____
_____
_____

Scripture/Subject _____

_____

My Thoughts _____

_____

_____

_____

_____

_____

_____

_____

_____

_____

_____

_____

_____

_____

_____

_____

_____

_____

_____

_____

_____

Faith Step for Today _____

_____

_____

_____

And he did not do many miracles there because of their lack of faith.
Matthew 13:58

DATE: _____

Scripture/Subject _____
_____

My Thoughts _____
_____
_____
_____
_____
_____
_____
_____
_____
_____
_____
_____
_____
_____
_____
_____
_____
_____
_____
_____

Faith Step for Today _____
_____
_____
_____

DATE: _____

Scripture/Subject _____
_____

My Thoughts _____
_____
_____
_____
_____
_____
_____
_____
_____
_____
_____
_____
_____
_____
_____
_____
_____
_____
_____
_____

Faith Step for Today _____
_____
_____
_____

Then Jesus said, "Did I not tell you that if you believed,
you would see the glory of God?"
John 11:40

13

DATE: _____

Scripture/Subject _____
_____

My Thoughts _____
_____
_____
_____
_____
_____
_____
_____
_____
_____
_____
_____
_____
_____
_____
_____
_____
_____
_____

Faith Step for Today _____
_____
_____
_____

DATE: _____

Scripture/Subject _____

_____

My Thoughts _____

_____

_____

_____

_____

_____

_____

_____

_____

_____

_____

_____

_____

_____

_____

_____

_____

_____

_____

_____

Faith Step for Today _____

_____

_____

_____

You will seek me and find me when you seek me with all your heart.
Jeremiah 29:13

DATE: _____

Scripture/Subject _____
_____

My Thoughts _____
_____
_____
_____
_____
_____
_____
_____
_____
_____
_____
_____
_____
_____
_____
_____
_____
_____
_____
_____
_____

Faith Step for Today _____
_____
_____
_____

Scripture/Subject _____
_____

My Thoughts _____
_____
_____
_____
_____
_____
_____
_____
_____
_____
_____
_____
_____
_____
_____
_____
_____
_____

Faith Step for Today _____
_____
_____
_____

And without faith it is impossible to please God, because anyone who comes to him
must believe that he exists and that he rewards those who earnestly seek him.
Hebrews 11:6

DATE: _____

Scripture/Subject _____
_____

My Thoughts _____
_____
_____
_____
_____
_____
_____
_____
_____
_____
_____
_____
_____
_____
_____
_____
_____
_____
_____
_____
_____
_____
_____

Faith Step for Today _____
_____
_____
_____

Scripture/Subject _____

_____

My Thoughts _____

_____

_____

_____

_____

_____

_____

_____

_____

_____

_____

_____

_____

_____

_____

_____

_____

_____

Faith Step for Today _____

_____

_____

_____

I tell you the truth, if you have faith as small as a mustard seed,
you can say to this mountain, "Move from here to there" and it will move.
Nothing will be impossible for you.
Matthew 17:20

DATE: _____

Scripture/Subject _____
_____

My Thoughts _____
_____
_____
_____
_____
_____
_____
_____
_____
_____
_____
_____
_____
_____
_____
_____
_____
_____
_____
_____

Faith Step for Today _____
_____
_____
_____

Scripture/Subject _____

_____

My Thoughts _____

_____

_____

_____

_____

_____

_____

_____

_____

_____

_____

_____

_____

_____

_____

_____

_____

_____

Faith Step for Today _____

_____

_____

_____

Who is it that overcomes the world?
Only he who believes that Jesus is the Son of God.
1 John 5:5

DATE: _____

Scripture/Subject _____
_____

My Thoughts _____
_____
_____
_____
_____
_____
_____
_____
_____
_____
_____
_____
_____
_____
_____
_____
_____
_____
_____
_____
_____
_____
_____

Faith Step for Today _____
_____
_____
_____

Scripture/Subject _____

_____

My Thoughts _____

_____

_____

_____

_____

_____

_____

_____

_____

_____

_____

_____

_____

_____

_____

_____

_____

_____

_____

Faith Step for Today _____

_____

_____

_____

He came as a witness to testify concerning that light,
so that through him all men might believe.
John 1:7

DATE: _____

Scripture/Subject _____
_____

My Thoughts _____
_____
_____
_____
_____
_____
_____
_____
_____
_____
_____
_____
_____
_____
_____
_____
_____
_____
_____
_____

Faith Step for Today _____
_____
_____
_____

DATE: _____

Scripture/Subject _____
_____

My Thoughts _____
_____
_____
_____
_____
_____
_____
_____
_____
_____
_____
_____
_____
_____
_____
_____
_____
_____
_____

Faith Step for Today _____
_____
_____
_____

This righteousness from God comes through faith in Jesus Christ to all who believe…
Romans 3:22

25

DATE: _____

Scripture/Subject _____
_____

My Thoughts _____
_____
_____
_____
_____
_____
_____
_____
_____
_____
_____
_____
_____
_____
_____
_____
_____
_____
_____
_____
_____
_____
_____

Faith Step for Today _____
_____
_____
_____

Scripture/Subject _____

_____

My Thoughts _____

_____

_____

_____

_____

_____

_____

_____

_____

_____

_____

_____

_____

_____

_____

_____

_____

_____

_____

_____

_____

Faith Step for Today _____

_____

_____

_____

We live by faith, not by sight.
2 Corinthians 5:7

DATE: _____

Scripture/Subject _____
_____

My Thoughts _____
_____
_____
_____
_____
_____
_____
_____
_____
_____
_____
_____
_____
_____
_____
_____
_____
_____
_____
_____
_____
_____
_____

Faith Step for Today _____
_____
_____
_____

Scripture/Subject _____
_____

My Thoughts _____
_____
_____
_____
_____
_____
_____
_____
_____
_____
_____
_____
_____
_____
_____
_____
_____
_____
_____
_____

Faith Step for Today _____
_____
_____
_____

Ask and it will be given to you; seek and you will find;
knock and the door will be opened to you.
Matthew 7:7

DATE: _____

Scripture/Subject _____
_____

My Thoughts _____
_____
_____
_____
_____
_____
_____
_____
_____
_____
_____
_____
_____
_____
_____
_____
_____
_____
_____
_____
_____

Faith Step for Today _____
_____
_____
_____

Scripture/Subject _____

_____

My Thoughts _____

_____

_____

_____

_____

_____

_____

_____

_____

_____

_____

_____

_____

_____

_____

_____

_____

_____

_____

_____

Faith Step for Today _____

_____

_____

_____

When my spirit grows faint within me, it is you who know my way...
Psalm 142:3

DATE: _____

Scripture/Subject _____
_____

My Thoughts _____
_____
_____
_____
_____
_____
_____
_____
_____
_____
_____
_____
_____
_____
_____
_____
_____
_____
_____
_____
_____
_____

Faith Step for Today _____
_____
_____
_____

Scripture/Subject _____
_____

My Thoughts _____
_____
_____
_____
_____
_____
_____
_____
_____
_____
_____
_____
_____
_____
_____
_____
_____
_____
_____
_____
_____

Faith Step for Today _____
_____
_____
_____

I am God Almighty; walk before me and be blameless.
Genesis 17:1

DATE: _____

Scripture/Subject _____
_____

My Thoughts _____
_____
_____
_____
_____
_____
_____
_____
_____
_____
_____
_____
_____
_____
_____
_____
_____
_____
_____
_____

Faith Step for Today _____
_____
_____
_____

Scripture/Subject _____
_____

My Thoughts _____
_____
_____
_____
_____
_____
_____
_____
_____
_____
_____
_____
_____
_____
_____
_____
_____
_____
_____
_____
_____
_____

Faith Step for Today _____
_____
_____
_____

All the prophets testify about him that everyone who believes in him
receives forgiveness of sins through his name.
Acts 10:43

DATE: _____

Scripture/Subject _____
_____

My Thoughts _____
_____
_____
_____
_____
_____
_____
_____
_____
_____
_____
_____
_____
_____
_____
_____
_____
_____
_____
_____
_____

Faith Step for Today _____
_____
_____
_____

Scripture/Subject _____
_____

My Thoughts _____
_____
_____
_____
_____
_____
_____
_____
_____
_____
_____
_____
_____
_____
_____
_____
_____

Faith Step for Today _____
_____
_____
_____

Fight the good fight of the faith.
Take hold of the eternal life to which you were called...
1 Timothy 6:12

DATE: _____

Scripture/Subject _____
_____

My Thoughts _____
_____
_____
_____
_____
_____
_____
_____
_____
_____
_____
_____
_____
_____
_____
_____
_____
_____
_____
_____
_____
_____

Faith Step for Today _____
_____
_____
_____

Scripture/Subject _____

_____

My Thoughts _____

_____

_____

_____

_____

_____

_____

_____

_____

_____

_____

_____

_____

_____

_____

_____

_____

_____

_____

_____

Faith Step for Today _____

_____

_____

_____

Then the man said, "Lord, I believe," and he worshiped him.
John 9:38

DATE: _____

Scripture/Subject _____
_____

My Thoughts _____
_____
_____
_____
_____
_____
_____
_____
_____
_____
_____
_____
_____
_____
_____
_____
_____
_____
_____
_____
_____
_____

Faith Step for Today _____
_____
_____
_____

Scripture/Subject _____

_____

My Thoughts _____

_____

_____

_____

_____

_____

_____

_____

_____

_____

_____

_____

_____

_____

_____

_____

_____

_____

_____

_____

_____

Faith Step for Today _____

_____

_____

_____

Yet he did not waver through unbelief regarding the promise of God,
but was strengthened in his faith and gave glory to God, being fully persuaded
that God had power to do what he had promised.
Romans 4:20-21

DATE: _____

Scripture/Subject _____
_____

My Thoughts _____
_____
_____
_____
_____
_____
_____
_____
_____
_____
_____
_____
_____
_____
_____
_____
_____
_____
_____
_____
_____
_____

Faith Step for Today _____
_____
_____
_____

Scripture/Subject _____

_____

My Thoughts _____

_____

_____

_____

_____

_____

_____

_____

_____

_____

_____

_____

_____

_____

_____

_____

_____

_____

_____

Faith Step for Today _____

_____

_____

_____

Now faith is being sure of what we hope for and certain of what we do not see.
Hebrews 11:1

DATE: _____

Scripture/Subject _____

_____

My Thoughts _____

_____

_____

_____

_____

_____

_____

_____

_____

_____

_____

_____

_____

_____

_____

_____

_____

_____

_____

_____

Faith Step for Today _____

_____

_____

_____

Scripture/Subject _____
_____

My Thoughts _____
_____
_____
_____
_____
_____
_____
_____
_____
_____
_____
_____
_____
_____
_____
_____
_____
_____
_____
_____

Faith Step for Today _____
_____
_____
_____

But you, dear friends, build yourselves up in your most holy faith
and pray in the Holy Spirit.
Jude 1:20

DATE: _____

Scripture/Subject _____
_____

My Thoughts _____
_____
_____
_____
_____
_____
_____
_____
_____
_____
_____
_____
_____
_____
_____
_____
_____
_____
_____
_____
_____
_____
_____

Faith Step for Today _____
_____
_____
_____

Scripture/Subject _____

_____

My Thoughts _____

_____

_____

_____

_____

_____

_____

_____

_____

_____

_____

_____

_____

_____

_____

_____

_____

_____

_____

_____

Faith Step for Today _____

_____

_____

_____

In addition to all this, take up the shield of faith, with which you can extinguish
all the flaming arrows of the evil one.
Ephesians 6:16

DATE: _____

Scripture/Subject _____
_____

My Thoughts _____
_____
_____
_____
_____
_____
_____
_____
_____
_____
_____
_____
_____
_____
_____
_____
_____
_____
_____
_____
_____
_____

Faith Step for Today _____
_____
_____
_____

Scripture/Subject _____

_____

My Thoughts _____

_____

_____

_____

_____

_____

_____

_____

_____

_____

_____

_____

_____

_____

_____

_____

_____

_____

Faith Step for Today _____

_____

_____

_____

Observe the commands of the LORD your God,
walking in his ways and revering him.
Deuteronomy 8:6

DATE: _____

Scripture/Subject _____
_____

My Thoughts _____
_____
_____
_____
_____
_____
_____
_____
_____
_____
_____
_____
_____
_____
_____
_____
_____
_____
_____
_____
_____

Faith Step for Today _____
_____
_____
_____

Scripture/Subject _____

_____

My Thoughts _____

_____

_____

_____

_____

_____

_____

_____

_____

_____

_____

_____

_____

_____

_____

_____

_____

_____

_____

_____

Faith Step for Today _____

_____

_____

_____

I am not ashamed of the gospel, because it is the power of God for the salvation
of everyone who believes: first for the Jew, then for the Gentile.
Romans 1:16

DATE: _____

Scripture/Subject _____
_____

My Thoughts _____
_____
_____
_____
_____
_____
_____
_____
_____
_____
_____
_____
_____
_____
_____
_____
_____
_____
_____

Faith Step for Today _____
_____
_____
_____

Scripture/Subject _____

_____

My Thoughts _____

_____

_____

_____

_____

_____

_____

_____

_____

_____

_____

_____

_____

_____

_____

_____

_____

Faith Step for Today _____

_____

_____

_____

Let love and faithfulness never leave you;
bind them around your neck,
write them on the tablet of your heart.
Proverbs 3:3

DATE: _____

Scripture/Subject _____
_____

My Thoughts _____
_____
_____
_____
_____
_____
_____
_____
_____
_____
_____
_____
_____
_____
_____
_____
_____
_____
_____

Faith Step for Today _____
_____
_____
_____

Scripture/Subject _____

_____

My Thoughts _____

_____

_____

_____

_____

_____

_____

_____

_____

_____

_____

_____

_____

_____

_____

_____

_____

_____

Faith Step for Today _____

_____

_____

_____

Immediately Jesus reached out his hand and caught him.
"You of little faith," he said, "why did you doubt?"
Matthew 14:31

DATE: _____

Scripture/Subject _____
_____

My Thoughts _____
_____
_____
_____
_____
_____
_____
_____
_____
_____
_____
_____
_____
_____
_____
_____
_____
_____
_____

Faith Step for Today _____
_____
_____
_____

DATE: _____

Scripture/Subject _____

_____

My Thoughts _____

_____

_____

_____

_____

_____

_____

_____

_____

_____

_____

_____

_____

_____

_____

_____

_____

_____

Faith Step for Today _____

_____

_____

_____

So keep up your courage, men, for I have faith in God
that it will happen just as he told me.
Acts 27:25

DATE: _____

Scripture/Subject _____

_____

My Thoughts _____

_____

_____

_____

_____

_____

_____

_____

_____

_____

_____

_____

_____

_____

_____

_____

_____

_____

_____

_____

Faith Step for Today _____

_____

_____

_____

Scripture/Subject _____

_____

My Thoughts _____

_____

_____

_____

_____

_____

_____

_____

_____

_____

_____

_____

_____

_____

_____

_____

_____

_____

_____

Faith Step for Today _____

_____

_____

_____

Abram believed the LORD, and he credited it to him as righteousness.
Genesis 15:6

DATE: _____

Scripture/Subject _____
_____

My Thoughts _____
_____
_____
_____
_____
_____
_____
_____
_____
_____
_____
_____
_____
_____
_____
_____
_____
_____
_____
_____
_____
_____

Faith Step for Today _____
_____
_____
_____

Scripture/Subject _____
_____

My Thoughts _____
_____
_____
_____
_____
_____
_____
_____
_____
_____
_____
_____
_____
_____
_____
_____
_____
_____
_____

Faith Step for Today _____
_____
_____
_____

He replied, "Blessed rather are those who hear the word of God and obey it."
Luke 11:28

DATE: _____

Scripture/Subject _____
_____

My Thoughts _____
_____
_____
_____
_____
_____
_____
_____
_____
_____
_____
_____
_____
_____
_____
_____
_____
_____
_____
_____
_____
_____
_____

Faith Step for Today _____
_____
_____
_____

Scripture/Subject _____

_____

My Thoughts _____

_____

_____

_____

_____

_____

_____

_____

_____

_____

_____

_____

_____

_____

_____

_____

_____

_____

Faith Step for Today _____

_____

_____

_____

For if those who live by the law are heirs,
faith has no value and the promise is worthless…
Romans 4:14

DATE: _____

Scripture/Subject _____
_____

My Thoughts _____
_____
_____
_____
_____
_____
_____
_____
_____
_____
_____
_____
_____
_____
_____
_____
_____
_____
_____
_____
_____
_____

Faith Step for Today _____
_____
_____
_____

Scripture/Subject _____

_____

My Thoughts _____

_____

_____

_____

_____

_____

_____

_____

_____

_____

_____

_____

_____

_____

_____

_____

_____

_____

_____

Faith Step for Today _____

_____

_____

_____

Do not merely listen to the word, and so deceive yourselves. Do what it says.
James 1:22

DATE: _____

Scripture/Subject _____
_____

My Thoughts _____
_____
_____
_____
_____
_____
_____
_____
_____
_____
_____
_____
_____
_____
_____
_____
_____
_____
_____
_____
_____

Faith Step for Today _____
_____
_____
_____

Scripture/Subject _____

_____

My Thoughts _____

_____

_____

_____

_____

_____

_____

_____

_____

_____

_____

_____

_____

_____

_____

_____

_____

_____

Faith Step for Today _____

_____

_____

_____

...for everyone born of God overcomes the world.
This is the victory that has overcome the world, even our faith.
1 John 5:4

DATE: _____

Scripture/Subject _____
_____

My Thoughts _____
_____
_____
_____
_____
_____
_____
_____
_____
_____
_____
_____
_____
_____
_____
_____
_____
_____
_____
_____
_____

Faith Step for Today _____
_____
_____
_____

Scripture/Subject _____
_____

My Thoughts _____
_____
_____
_____
_____
_____
_____
_____
_____
_____
_____
_____
_____
_____
_____
_____
_____
_____
_____
_____
_____
_____
_____
_____

Faith Step for Today _____
_____
_____
_____

Then Jesus told him, "Because you have seen me, you have believed;
blessed are those who have not seen and yet have believed."
John 20:29

DATE: _____

Scripture/Subject _____
_____

My Thoughts _____
_____
_____
_____
_____
_____
_____
_____
_____
_____
_____
_____
_____
_____
_____
_____
_____
_____
_____
_____

Faith Step for Today _____
_____
_____
_____

Scripture/Subject _____

_____

My Thoughts _____

_____

_____

_____

_____

_____

_____

_____

_____

_____

_____

_____

_____

_____

_____

_____

_____

_____

Faith Step for Today _____

_____

_____

_____

If that is how God clothes the grass of the field, which is here today
and tomorrow is thrown into the fire, will he not much more clothe you,
O you of little faith?
Matthew 6:30

DATE: _____

Scripture/Subject _____
_____

My Thoughts _____
_____
_____
_____
_____
_____
_____
_____
_____
_____
_____
_____
_____
_____
_____
_____
_____
_____
_____

Faith Step for Today _____
_____
_____
_____

Scripture/Subject _____
_____

My Thoughts _____
_____
_____
_____
_____
_____
_____
_____
_____
_____
_____
_____
_____
_____
_____
_____
_____
_____
_____

Faith Step for Today _____
_____
_____
_____

For God so loved the world that he gave his one and only Son,
that whoever believes in him shall not perish but have eternal life.
John 3:16

DATE: _____

Scripture/Subject _____
_____

My Thoughts _____
_____
_____
_____
_____
_____
_____
_____
_____
_____
_____
_____
_____
_____
_____
_____
_____
_____
_____
_____
_____

Faith Step for Today _____
_____
_____
_____

Scripture/Subject _____
_____

My Thoughts _____
_____
_____
_____
_____
_____
_____
_____
_____
_____
_____
_____
_____
_____
_____
_____
_____
_____
_____
_____

Faith Step for Today _____
_____
_____
_____

And when they heard that the LORD was concerned about them
and had seen their misery, they bowed down and worshiped.
Exodus 4:31

DATE: _____

Scripture/Subject _____
_____

My Thoughts _____
_____
_____
_____
_____
_____
_____
_____
_____
_____
_____
_____
_____
_____
_____
_____
_____
_____
_____
_____
_____
_____

Faith Step for Today _____
_____
_____
_____

Scripture/Subject _____
_____

My Thoughts _____
_____
_____
_____
_____
_____
_____
_____
_____
_____
_____
_____
_____
_____
_____
_____
_____
_____

Faith Step for Today _____
_____
_____
_____

What if some did not have faith?
Will their lack of faith nullify God's faithfulness?
Romans 3:3

DATE: _____

Scripture/Subject _____
_____

My Thoughts _____
_____
_____
_____
_____
_____
_____
_____
_____
_____
_____
_____
_____
_____
_____
_____
_____
_____
_____
_____
_____
_____

Faith Step for Today _____
_____
_____
_____

Scripture/Subject _____

_____

My Thoughts _____

_____

_____

_____

_____

_____

_____

_____

_____

_____

_____

_____

_____

_____

_____

_____

_____

_____

_____

_____

_____

_____

Faith Step for Today _____

_____

_____

_____

I have spoken to you of earthly things and you do not believe;
how then will you believe if I speak of heavenly things?
John 3:12

DATE: _____

Scripture/Subject _____
_____

My Thoughts _____
_____
_____
_____
_____
_____
_____
_____
_____
_____
_____
_____
_____
_____
_____
_____
_____
_____
_____
_____
_____
_____

Faith Step for Today _____
_____
_____
_____

Scripture/Subject _____

_____

My Thoughts _____

_____

_____

_____

_____

_____

_____

_____

_____

_____

_____

_____

_____

_____

_____

_____

_____

_____

_____

Faith Step for Today _____

_____

_____

_____

For we also have had the gospel preached to us, just as they did;
but the message they heard was of no value to them,
because those who heard did not combine it with faith.
Hebrews 4:2

DATE: _____

Scripture/Subject _____
_____

My Thoughts _____
_____
_____
_____
_____
_____
_____
_____
_____
_____
_____
_____
_____
_____
_____
_____
_____
_____
_____
_____
_____

Faith Step for Today _____
_____
_____
_____

DATE: _____

Scripture/Subject _____
_____

My Thoughts _____
_____
_____
_____
_____
_____
_____
_____
_____
_____
_____
_____
_____
_____
_____
_____
_____
_____
_____
_____
_____
_____

Faith Step for Today _____
_____
_____
_____

...if you confess with your mouth, "Jesus is Lord," and believe in your heart
that God raised him from the dead, you will be saved.
Romans 10:9

DATE: _____

Scripture/Subject _____
_____

My Thoughts _____
_____
_____
_____
_____
_____
_____
_____
_____
_____
_____
_____
_____
_____
_____
_____
_____
_____
_____
_____
_____
_____

Faith Step for Today _____
_____
_____
_____

Scripture/Subject _____

_____

My Thoughts _____

_____

_____

_____

_____

_____

_____

_____

_____

_____

_____

_____

_____

_____

_____

_____

_____

_____

_____

_____

_____

Faith Step for Today _____

_____

_____

_____

…you know that the testing of your faith develops perseverance.
James 1:3

DATE: _____

Scripture/Subject _____
_____

My Thoughts _____
_____
_____
_____
_____
_____
_____
_____
_____
_____
_____
_____
_____
_____
_____
_____
_____
_____
_____
_____

Faith Step for Today _____
_____
_____
_____

Scripture/Subject _____

_____

My Thoughts _____

_____

_____

_____

_____

_____

_____

_____

_____

_____

_____

_____

_____

_____

_____

_____

_____

Faith Step for Today _____

_____

_____

_____

Jesus told the synagogue ruler, "Don't be afraid; just believe."
Mark 5:36

DATE: _____

Scripture/Subject _____
_____

My Thoughts _____
_____
_____
_____
_____
_____
_____
_____
_____
_____
_____
_____
_____
_____
_____
_____
_____
_____
_____
_____
_____
_____

Faith Step for Today _____
_____
_____
_____

DATE: _____

Scripture/Subject _____
_____

My Thoughts _____
_____
_____
_____
_____
_____
_____
_____
_____
_____
_____
_____
_____
_____
_____
_____
_____
_____
_____
_____
_____

Faith Step for Today _____
_____
_____
_____

But since we belong to the day, let us be self-controlled, putting on faith
and love as a breastplate, and the hope of salvation as a helmet.
1 Thessalonians 5:8

DATE: _____

Scripture/Subject _____
_____

My Thoughts _____
_____
_____
_____
_____
_____
_____
_____
_____
_____
_____
_____
_____
_____
_____
_____
_____
_____
_____
_____
_____
_____
_____
_____

Faith Step for Today _____
_____
_____
_____

Scripture/Subject _____
_____

My Thoughts _____
_____
_____
_____
_____
_____
_____
_____
_____
_____
_____
_____
_____
_____
_____
_____
_____
_____
_____

Faith Step for Today _____
_____
_____
_____

For it is by grace you have been saved, through faith—and this not from yourselves,
it is the gift of God—not by works, so that no one can boast.
Ephesians 2:8-9

DATE: _____

Scripture/Subject _____
_____

My Thoughts _____
_____
_____
_____
_____
_____
_____
_____
_____
_____
_____
_____
_____
_____
_____
_____
_____
_____
_____
_____
_____
_____
_____

Faith Step for Today _____
_____
_____
_____

Scripture/Subject _____

_____

My Thoughts _____

_____

_____

_____

_____

_____

_____

_____

_____

_____

_____

_____

_____

_____

_____

_____

_____

Faith Step for Today _____

_____

_____

_____

Then Jesus answered, "Woman, you have great faith! Your request is granted."
Matthew 15:28

DATE: _____

Scripture/Subject _____
_____

My Thoughts _____
_____
_____
_____
_____
_____
_____
_____
_____
_____
_____
_____
_____
_____
_____
_____
_____
_____
_____
_____

Faith Step for Today _____
_____
_____
_____

DATE: _____

Scripture/Subject _____
_____

My Thoughts _____
_____
_____
_____
_____
_____
_____
_____
_____
_____
_____
_____
_____
_____
_____
_____
_____
_____
_____
_____
_____

Faith Step for Today _____
_____
_____
_____

But when he asks, he must believe and not doubt, because he who doubts
is like a wave of the sea, blown and tossed by the wind.
James 1:6

DATE: _____

Scripture/Subject _____

_____

My Thoughts _____

_____

_____

_____

_____

_____

_____

_____

_____

_____

_____

_____

_____

_____

_____

_____

_____

_____

_____

_____

_____

_____

Faith Step for Today _____

_____

_____

_____

Scripture/Subject _____
_____

My Thoughts _____
_____
_____
_____
_____
_____
_____
_____
_____
_____
_____
_____
_____
_____
_____
_____
_____
_____
_____
_____

Faith Step for Today _____
_____
_____
_____

I know whom I have believed, and am convinced that he is able to guard
what I have entrusted to him for that day.
2 Timothy 1:12

DATE: _____

Scripture/Subject _____
_____

My Thoughts _____
_____
_____
_____
_____
_____
_____
_____
_____
_____
_____
_____
_____
_____
_____
_____
_____
_____
_____
_____
_____

Faith Step for Today _____
_____
_____
_____

Scripture/Subject _____
_____

My Thoughts _____
_____
_____
_____
_____
_____
_____
_____
_____
_____
_____
_____
_____
_____
_____
_____
_____
_____

Faith Step for Today _____
_____
_____
_____

...anyone who has faith in me will do what I have been doing.
He will do even greater things than these, because I am going to the Father.
John 14:12

DATE: _____

Scripture/Subject _____
_____

My Thoughts _____
_____
_____
_____
_____
_____
_____
_____
_____
_____
_____
_____
_____
_____
_____
_____
_____
_____
_____
_____
_____
_____

Faith Step for Today _____
_____
_____
_____

Scripture/Subject _____
_____

My Thoughts _____
_____
_____
_____
_____
_____
_____
_____
_____
_____
_____
_____
_____
_____
_____
_____
_____
_____
_____
_____
_____
_____

Faith Step for Today _____
_____
_____
_____

However, to the man who does not work but trusts God who justifies the wicked,
his faith is credited as righteousness.
Romans 4:5

DATE: _____

Scripture/Subject _____
_____

My Thoughts _____
_____
_____
_____
_____
_____
_____
_____
_____
_____
_____
_____
_____
_____
_____
_____
_____
_____
_____
_____
_____

Faith Step for Today _____
_____
_____
_____

Scripture/Subject _____
_____

My Thoughts _____
_____
_____
_____
_____
_____
_____
_____
_____
_____
_____
_____
_____
_____
_____
_____
_____
_____
_____
_____
_____
_____
_____

Faith Step for Today _____
_____
_____
_____

Then they believed his promises and sang his praise.
Psalm 106:12

DATE: _____

Scripture/Subject _____
_____

My Thoughts _____
_____
_____
_____
_____
_____
_____
_____
_____
_____
_____
_____
_____
_____
_____
_____
_____
_____
_____

Faith Step for Today _____
_____
_____
_____

Scripture/Subject _____

_____

My Thoughts _____

_____

_____

_____

_____

_____

_____

_____

_____

_____

_____

_____

_____

_____

_____

_____

_____

_____

_____

_____

Faith Step for Today _____

_____

_____

_____

Then Jesus declared, "I am the bread of life. He who comes to me will never go hungry,
and he who believes in me will never be thirsty."
John 6:35

DATE: _____

Scripture/Subject _____

_____

My Thoughts _____

_____

_____

_____

_____

_____

_____

_____

_____

_____

_____

_____

_____

_____

_____

_____

_____

_____

_____

_____

Faith Step for Today _____

_____

_____

_____

Scripture/Subject _____

_____

My Thoughts _____

_____

_____

_____

_____

_____

_____

_____

_____

_____

_____

_____

_____

_____

_____

_____

_____

_____

_____

_____

Faith Step for Today _____

_____

_____

_____

If I have the gift of prophecy and can fathom all mysteries and all knowledge,
and if I have a faith that can move mountains, and have not love, I am nothing.
1 Corinthians 13:2

DATE: _____

Scripture/Subject _____
_____

My Thoughts _____
_____
_____
_____
_____
_____
_____
_____
_____
_____
_____
_____
_____
_____
_____
_____
_____
_____
_____
_____

Faith Step for Today _____
_____
_____
_____

DATE: _____

Scripture/Subject _____
_____

My Thoughts _____
_____
_____
_____
_____
_____
_____
_____
_____
_____
_____
_____
_____
_____
_____
_____
_____
_____
_____
_____
_____

Faith Step for Today _____
_____
_____
_____

Blessed is she who has believed that what the Lord
has said to her will be accomplished!
Luke 1:45

DATE: _____

Scripture/Subject _____
_____

My Thoughts _____
_____
_____
_____
_____
_____
_____
_____
_____
_____
_____
_____
_____
_____
_____
_____
_____
_____
_____

Faith Step for Today _____
_____
_____
_____

Scripture/Subject _____
_____

My Thoughts _____
_____
_____
_____
_____
_____
_____
_____
_____
_____
_____
_____
_____
_____
_____
_____
_____
_____
_____

Faith Step for Today _____
_____
_____
_____

Then he touched their eyes and said,
"According to your faith will it be done to you";
and their sight was restored.
Matthew 9:29-30

DATE: _____

Scripture/Subject _____
_____

My Thoughts _____
_____
_____
_____
_____
_____
_____
_____
_____
_____
_____
_____
_____
_____
_____
_____
_____
_____
_____
_____
_____
_____
_____

Faith Step for Today _____
_____
_____
_____

Scripture/Subject _____

_____

My Thoughts _____

_____

_____

_____

_____

_____

_____

_____

_____

_____

_____

_____

_____

_____

_____

_____

_____

_____

_____

Faith Step for Today _____

_____

_____

_____

Test me, O LORD, and try me, examine my heart and my mind;
for your love is ever before me, and I walk continually in your truth.
Psalm 26:2-4

DATE: _____

Scripture/Subject _____
_____

My Thoughts _____
_____
_____
_____
_____
_____
_____
_____
_____
_____
_____
_____
_____
_____
_____
_____
_____
_____
_____
_____
_____
_____

Faith Step for Today _____
_____
_____
_____

Scripture/Subject _____

_____

My Thoughts _____

_____

_____

_____

_____

_____

_____

_____

_____

_____

_____

_____

_____

_____

_____

_____

_____

_____

_____

Faith Step for Today _____

_____

_____

_____

I have declared to both Jews and Greeks that they must turn to God
in repentance and have faith in our Lord Jesus.
Acts 20:21

DATE: _____

Scripture/Subject _____
_____

My Thoughts _____
_____
_____
_____
_____
_____
_____
_____
_____
_____
_____
_____
_____
_____
_____
_____
_____
_____
_____
_____

Faith Step for Today _____
_____
_____
_____

Scripture/Subject _____
_____

My Thoughts _____
_____
_____
_____
_____
_____
_____
_____
_____
_____
_____
_____
_____
_____
_____
_____
_____
_____

Faith Step for Today _____
_____
_____
_____

...when you received the word of God, which you heard from us,
you accepted it not as the word of men, but as it actually is, the word of God,
which is at work in you who believe.
1 Thessalonians 2:13

DATE: _____

Scripture/Subject _____
_____

My Thoughts _____
_____
_____
_____
_____
_____
_____
_____
_____
_____
_____
_____
_____
_____
_____
_____
_____
_____
_____
_____

Faith Step for Today _____
_____
_____
_____

Scripture/Subject _____

_____

My Thoughts _____

_____

_____

_____

_____

_____

_____

_____

_____

_____

_____

_____

_____

_____

_____

_____

_____

_____

_____

_____

_____

Faith Step for Today _____

_____

_____

_____

Call to me and I will answer you and tell you great
and unsearchable things you do not know.
Jeremiah 33:3

DATE: _____

Scripture/Subject _____

_____

My Thoughts _____

_____

_____

_____

_____

_____

_____

_____

_____

_____

_____

_____

_____

_____

_____

_____

_____

Faith Step for Today _____

_____

_____

_____

Scripture/Subject _____

_____

My Thoughts _____

_____

_____

_____

_____

_____

_____

_____

_____

_____

_____

_____

_____

_____

_____

_____

_____

_____

Faith Step for Today _____

_____

_____

_____

Does God give you his Spirit and work miracles among you
because you observe the law, or because you believe what you heard?
Galatians 3:5

DATE: _____

Scripture/Subject _____
_____

My Thoughts _____
_____
_____
_____
_____
_____
_____
_____
_____
_____
_____
_____
_____
_____
_____
_____
_____
_____
_____
_____
_____
_____
_____

Faith Step for Today _____
_____
_____
_____

DATE: _____

Scripture/Subject _____
_____

My Thoughts _____
_____
_____
_____
_____
_____
_____
_____
_____
_____
_____
_____
_____
_____
_____
_____
_____
_____
_____
_____

Faith Step for Today _____
_____
_____
_____

Believe in the Lord Jesus, and you will be saved—you and your household.
Acts 16:31

DATE: _____

Scripture/Subject _____
_____

My Thoughts _____
_____
_____
_____
_____
_____
_____
_____
_____
_____
_____
_____
_____
_____
_____
_____
_____
_____
_____
_____
_____

Faith Step for Today _____
_____
_____
_____

Scripture/Subject _____
_____

My Thoughts _____
_____
_____
_____
_____
_____
_____
_____
_____
_____
_____
_____
_____
_____
_____
_____
_____
_____
_____

Faith Step for Today _____
_____
_____
_____

But we are not of those who shrink back and are destroyed,
but of those who believe and are saved.
Hebrews 10:39

DATE: _____

Scripture/Subject _____
_____

My Thoughts _____
_____
_____
_____
_____
_____
_____
_____
_____
_____
_____
_____
_____
_____
_____
_____
_____
_____
_____
_____
_____
_____
_____

Faith Step for Today _____
_____
_____
_____

Scripture/Subject _____

_____

My Thoughts _____

_____

_____

_____

_____

_____

_____

_____

_____

_____

_____

_____

_____

_____

_____

_____

_____

Faith Step for Today _____

_____

_____

_____

I have been crucified with Christ and I no longer live, but Christ lives in me.
The life I live in the body, I live by faith in the Son of God,
who loved me and gave himself for me.
Galatians 2:20

DATE: _____

Scripture/Subject _____

_____

My Thoughts _____

_____

_____

_____

_____

_____

_____

_____

_____

_____

_____

_____

_____

_____

_____

_____

_____

_____

_____

_____

_____

_____

_____

Faith Step for Today _____

_____

_____

_____

Scripture/Subject _____

_____

My Thoughts _____

_____

_____

_____

_____

_____

_____

_____

_____

_____

_____

_____

_____

_____

_____

_____

_____

Faith Step for Today _____

_____

_____

_____

Therefore, since we have been justified through faith,
we have peace with God through our Lord Jesus Christ.
Romans 5:1

DATE: _____

Scripture/Subject _____
_____

My Thoughts _____
_____
_____
_____
_____
_____
_____
_____
_____
_____
_____
_____
_____
_____
_____
_____
_____
_____
_____

Faith Step for Today _____
_____
_____
_____

Scripture/Subject _____
_____

My Thoughts _____
_____
_____
_____
_____
_____
_____
_____
_____
_____
_____
_____
_____
_____
_____
_____
_____
_____
_____
_____
_____
_____

Faith Step for Today _____
_____
_____
_____

...when the Son of Man comes, will he find faith on the earth?
Luke 18:8

DATE: _____

Scripture/Subject _____
_____

My Thoughts _____
_____
_____
_____
_____
_____
_____
_____
_____
_____
_____
_____
_____
_____
_____
_____
_____
_____
_____
_____
_____
_____

Faith Step for Today _____
_____
_____
_____

Scripture/Subject _____

_____

My Thoughts _____

_____

_____

_____

_____

_____

_____

_____

_____

_____

_____

_____

_____

_____

_____

_____

_____

_____

Faith Step for Today _____

_____

_____

Immediately the boy's father exclaimed,
"I do believe; help me overcome my unbelief!"
Mark 9:24

DATE: _____

Scripture/Subject _____
_____

My Thoughts _____
_____
_____
_____
_____
_____
_____
_____
_____
_____
_____
_____
_____
_____
_____
_____
_____
_____

Faith Step for Today _____
_____
_____
_____

DATE: _____

Scripture/Subject _____
_____

My Thoughts _____
_____
_____
_____
_____
_____
_____
_____
_____
_____
_____
_____
_____
_____
_____
_____
_____
_____
_____
_____
_____
_____
_____

Faith Step for Today _____
_____
_____
_____

…let us draw near to God with a sincere heart in full assurance of faith…
Hebrews 10:22

DATE: _____

Scripture/Subject _____
_____

My Thoughts _____
_____
_____
_____
_____
_____
_____
_____
_____
_____
_____
_____
_____
_____
_____
_____
_____
_____
_____
_____

Faith Step for Today _____
_____
_____
_____

DATE: _____

Scripture/Subject _____
_____

My Thoughts _____
_____
_____
_____
_____
_____
_____
_____
_____
_____
_____
_____
_____
_____
_____
_____
_____
_____
_____

Faith Step for Today _____
_____
_____
_____

Consequently, faith comes from hearing the message,
and the message is heard through the word of Christ.
Romans 10:17

DATE: _____

Scripture/Subject _____

_____

My Thoughts _____

_____

_____

_____

_____

_____

_____

_____

_____

_____

_____

_____

_____

_____

_____

_____

_____

_____

_____

Faith Step for Today _____

_____

_____

_____

Scripture/Subject _____

_____

My Thoughts _____

_____

_____

_____

_____

_____

_____

_____

_____

_____

_____

_____

_____

_____

_____

_____

_____

_____

_____

Faith Step for Today _____

_____

_____

And he was amazed at their lack of faith.
Mark 6:6

DATE: _____

Scripture/Subject _____

_____

My Thoughts _____

_____

_____

_____

_____

_____

_____

_____

_____

_____

_____

_____

_____

_____

_____

_____

_____

_____

_____

Faith Step for Today _____

_____

_____

_____

Scripture/Subject _____

_____

My Thoughts _____

_____

_____

_____

_____

_____

_____

_____

_____

_____

_____

_____

_____

_____

_____

_____

_____

_____

_____

_____

_____

Faith Step for Today _____

_____

_____

_____

Jesus answered, "The work of God is this: to believe in the one he has sent."
John 6:29

DATE: _____

Scripture/Subject _____

_____

My Thoughts _____

_____

_____

_____

_____

_____

_____

_____

_____

_____

_____

_____

_____

_____

_____

_____

_____

_____

_____

_____

_____

Faith Step for Today _____

_____

_____

_____

Scripture/Subject _____

_____

My Thoughts _____

_____

_____

_____

_____

_____

_____

_____

_____

_____

_____

_____

_____

_____

_____

_____

Faith Step for Today _____

_____

_____

Through him everyone who believes is justified from everything
you could not be justified from by the law of Moses.
Acts 13:39

DATE: _____

Scripture/Subject _____
_____

My Thoughts _____
_____
_____
_____
_____
_____
_____
_____
_____
_____
_____
_____
_____
_____
_____
_____
_____
_____
_____
_____
_____
_____

Faith Step for Today _____
_____
_____
_____

Scripture/Subject _____

_____

My Thoughts _____

_____

_____

_____

_____

_____

_____

_____

_____

_____

_____

_____

_____

_____

_____

Faith Step for Today _____

_____

_____

_____

My message and my preaching were not with wise and persuasive words,
but with a demonstration of the Spirit's power, so that your faith might not rest
on men's wisdom, but on God's power.
1 Corinthians 2:4-5

DATE: _____

Scripture/Subject _____

_____

My Thoughts _____

_____

_____

_____

_____

_____

_____

_____

_____

_____

_____

_____

_____

_____

_____

_____

_____

_____

_____

_____

Faith Step for Today _____

_____

_____

_____

Scripture/Subject _____

_____

My Thoughts _____

_____

_____

_____

_____

_____

_____

_____

_____

_____

_____

_____

_____

_____

_____

_____

_____

_____

_____

Faith Step for Today _____

_____

_____

_____

…Well done, good and faithful servant! You have been faithful with a few things;
I will put you in charge of many things.
Matthew 25:21

DATE: _____

Scripture/Subject _____
_____

My Thoughts _____
_____
_____
_____
_____
_____
_____
_____
_____
_____
_____
_____
_____
_____
_____
_____
_____
_____
_____
_____

Faith Step for Today _____
_____
_____
_____

Scripture/Subject _____

_____

My Thoughts _____

_____

_____

_____

_____

_____

_____

_____

_____

_____

_____

_____

_____

_____

_____

_____

_____

_____

Faith Step for Today _____

_____

_____

_____

We do not want you to become lazy, but to imitate those who through faith
and patience inherit what has been promised.
Hebrews 6:12

DATE: _____

Scripture/Subject _____
_____

My Thoughts _____
_____
_____
_____
_____
_____
_____
_____
_____
_____
_____
_____
_____
_____
_____
_____
_____
_____
_____
_____
_____
_____
_____

Faith Step for Today _____
_____
_____
_____

Scripture/Subject _____
_____

My Thoughts _____
_____
_____
_____
_____
_____
_____
_____
_____
_____
_____
_____
_____
_____
_____
_____
_____
_____
_____

Faith Step for Today _____
_____
_____
_____

And if Christ has not been raised, our preaching is useless and so is your faith.
1 Corinthians 15:14

DATE: _____

Scripture/Subject _____
_____

My Thoughts _____
_____
_____
_____
_____
_____
_____
_____
_____
_____
_____
_____
_____
_____
_____
_____
_____
_____
_____
_____
_____
_____

Faith Step for Today _____
_____
_____
_____

Scripture/Subject _____
_____

My Thoughts _____
_____
_____
_____
_____
_____
_____
_____
_____
_____
_____
_____
_____
_____
_____
_____
_____
_____
_____

Faith Step for Today _____
_____
_____
_____

Teach me knowledge and good judgment, for I believe in your commands.
Psalm 119:66

DATE: _____

Scripture/Subject _____
_____

My Thoughts _____
_____
_____
_____
_____
_____
_____
_____
_____
_____
_____
_____
_____
_____
_____
_____
_____
_____
_____
_____

Faith Step for Today _____
_____
_____
_____

DATE: _____

Scripture/Subject _____

_____

My Thoughts _____

_____

_____

_____

_____

_____

_____

_____

_____

_____

_____

_____

_____

_____

_____

_____

_____

_____

_____

_____

_____

Faith Step for Today _____

_____

_____

_____

You believe that there is one God.
Good! Even the demons believe that—and shudder.
James 2:19

DATE: _____

Scripture/Subject _____
_____

My Thoughts _____
_____
_____
_____
_____
_____
_____
_____
_____
_____
_____
_____
_____
_____
_____
_____
_____
_____
_____
_____
_____
_____

Faith Step for Today _____
_____
_____
_____

Scripture/Subject _____

_____

My Thoughts _____

_____

_____

_____

_____

_____

_____

_____

_____

_____

_____

_____

_____

_____

_____

_____

_____

Faith Step for Today _____

_____

_____

_____

For in the gospel a righteousness from God is revealed,
a righteousness that is by faith from first to last, just as it is written:
"The righteous will live by faith."
Romans 1:17

DATE: _____

Scripture/Subject _____
_____

My Thoughts _____
_____
_____
_____
_____
_____
_____
_____
_____
_____
_____
_____
_____
_____
_____
_____
_____
_____
_____
_____
_____

Faith Step for Today _____
_____
_____
_____

DATE: _____

Scripture/Subject _____
_____

My Thoughts _____
_____
_____
_____
_____
_____
_____
_____
_____
_____
_____
_____
_____
_____
_____
_____
_____
_____
_____
_____

Faith Step for Today _____
_____
_____
_____

Even as he spoke, many put their faith in him.
John 8:30

DATE: _____

Scripture/Subject _____
_____

My Thoughts _____
_____
_____
_____
_____
_____
_____
_____
_____
_____
_____
_____
_____
_____
_____
_____
_____
_____
_____
_____
_____

Faith Step for Today _____
_____
_____
_____

Scripture/Subject _____

_____

My Thoughts _____

_____

_____

_____

_____

_____

_____

_____

_____

_____

_____

_____

_____

_____

_____

_____

_____

_____

_____

Faith Step for Today _____

_____

_____

_____

Be on your guard; stand firm in the faith; be men of courage; be strong.
1 Corinthians 16:13

DATE: _____

Scripture/Subject _____
_____

My Thoughts _____
_____
_____
_____
_____
_____
_____
_____
_____
_____
_____
_____
_____
_____
_____
_____
_____
_____
_____

Faith Step for Today _____
_____
_____
_____

Scripture/Subject _____

_____

My Thoughts _____

_____

_____

_____

_____

_____

_____

_____

_____

_____

_____

_____

_____

_____

_____

_____

_____

_____

_____

Faith Step for Today _____

_____

_____

_____

In him and through faith in him we may approach God
with freedom and confidence.
Ephesians 3:12

DATE: _____

Scripture/Subject _____
_____

My Thoughts _____
_____
_____
_____
_____
_____
_____
_____
_____
_____
_____
_____
_____
_____
_____
_____
_____
_____
_____
_____

Faith Step for Today _____
_____
_____
_____

DATE: _____

Scripture/Subject _____

_____

My Thoughts _____

_____

_____

_____

_____

_____

_____

_____

_____

_____

_____

_____

_____

_____

_____

_____

_____

_____

_____

_____

Faith Step for Today _____

_____

_____

_____

Let us fix our eyes on Jesus, the author and perfecter of our faith…
Hebrews 12:2

DATE: _____

Scripture/Subject _____
_____

My Thoughts _____
_____
_____
_____
_____
_____
_____
_____
_____
_____
_____
_____
_____
_____
_____
_____
_____
_____
_____
_____

Faith Step for Today _____
_____
_____
_____

PRAYER LIST

The prayer of a righteous man is powerful and effective.
James 5:16